THE HAMPTONS

THE HAMPTONS

LONG ISLAND'S EAST END

PHOTOGRAPHS BY KEN MILLER

INTRODUCTION BY GEORGE PLIMPTON

RIZZOLI
NEW YORK

Page 1: Garden, Southampton.

Pages 2–3: The oldest existing farmhouses in East Hampton:
Mulford House (left), built in 1680, is now owned by the Southampton Historical Society; the seventeenth–century farmhouse Home Sweet Home (right) takes its name from the song by John Howard Payne, who once resided there.

Page 4: Fence, East Hampton.

Pages 6–7: Flower farm, East Hampton.

Pages 10–11: Sunstone, residence, designed by Robert A. M. Stern, 1984–1987, East Quogue.

Pages 12–13: Georgica Beach, East Hampton.

Pages 18–19: Barn, Bridgehampton.

Pages 22–23: Windsurfers, Napeague Harbor.

First published in the United States of America in 1993 by
RIZZOLI INTERNATIONAL PUBLICATIONS, INC.
300 Park Avenue South, New York, NY 10010

Library of Congress Cataloging–in–Publication Data

Miller, Ken, 1963–
　　The Hamptons : Long Island's east end / photographs by
　Ken Miller ; introduction by George Plimpton.
　　　　p.　cm.
　　ISBN 0-8478-1694-X
　　1. Suffolk County (N.Y.)–Pictorial works. 2. Hamptons (N.Y.)–
　Pictorial works. 3. Architecture, Domestic–New York (State)–
　Hamptons–Pictorial works. I. Title.
　F127.S9M55　1993
　974.7'25–dc20　　　　　　　　　　　　　　　　　93–150
　　　　　　　　　　　　　　　　　　　　　　　　　　　　CIP

Designed by Gilda Hannah
Map by T. R. Lundquist
Printed in Singapore

For Patricia and Philip Miller

LONG ISLAND'S EAST END

Long Island Sound

Orient Point

Gardiners Bay

Gardiners Island

NORTH FORK

Shelter Island

Little Peconic Bay

Napeague Bay

Montauk Point

Robins Island

Sag Harbor

SOUTH FORK

Springs

Great Peconic Bay

Montauk

← TO NEW YORK CITY

East Hampton

Amagansett

Bridgehampton

Water Mill

Georgica

Hampton Bays

Southampton

Wainscott

Westhampton

Sagaponack

Quogue

Westhampton Beach

Atlantic Ocean

0   5   10

MILES

INTRODUCTION

I have been fortunate enough to live in a number of places in the Hamptons over the years. In the 1960s, before the Long Island Expressway was extended, we drove there by Horse Block Road, through Riverhead, and out past the Big Duck, the oversize replica that stood outrageously close to the highway, vacant–eyed, yellow–beaked, with a little door in its chest through which one went in to buy Long Island duck, though I never did, and I don't know any-body else who did either. The Big Duck was important because it was the landmark that meant New York City was far behind and we were almost home. "Thar she blows," we'd cry happily, and we'd sail on by.

The first ducks, incidentally, arrived in Long Island in 1873 on a clipper ship from China. Origi-nally called Peking duck, they were plump, white, fecund, a favorite of restaurateurs. I have been told that six million ducks at a time lived out their brief lives in the Hamptons—acreages of white forms waiting in the flat powdery dust for their ends. One of the farms was just outside Bridgehampton on Route 27—"Duckenwald" one of my friends called the gloomy place. The increase of land val-ues as the well–to–do migrated to summer homes meant the end of the duck operations, at least along the highways. The duck people tried to hang on—one of them taking desperate exception to those who criticized the acrid smell rising off the duck farms by calling it "healthy."

Those first years we rented summer houses in the Hamptons as if to test the varied possibilities before settling on a final choice. We started in Southampton, first in a beach house on Dune Road, perched on stilts on the backside of a dune, with a steep, wooden stairway that led up to the rear door, so that guests, especially if they were carrying luggage for a weekend stay, arrived pant-ing and flush–faced. A bay window looked out on the sea. It was a short walk through the saw–grass down to the beach and the water, and the guests tended to head for it before unpacking. Up the road toward town were the more traditional turn-of-the-century summer homes, gray-shingled, weathered by the storms, large, rambling. Further inland, the homes were more stately, many of them in seclusion behind the tall privet hedges that Southampton is noted for: thick and often as perfectly clipped and groomed as a show-poodle's tail. That summer we were invited to the ram-shackle Cutting house by the sea, and sitting in big white wicker chairs on the veranda, we heard the radio broadcast of the first landing on the moon.

The next year we went a mile or so east, still in Southampton, and spent the summer months in a sweltering apartment over a garage on Gin Lane. From the window it was possible to see the ocean over the dunes. Stretching to the base of the dunes was a great lawn on which we played croquet on the weekends and flew kites. We discovered the delicate Siamese fighting kites that with practice we could gyrate in the sky and in a strong breeze dive them, fluttering violently, within a foot of the ground and pull them skyward at that last instant. I remember an enormous box kite that we sent up in the evening, moored to a stick, and when the wind slackened that night, the kite dropped into the sea far beyond the breakers. The next morning its string stretched the length of the lawn, over the dunes, across the beach and into the surf as if a lazy fisherman had deserted his line in the middle of the lawn and gone home.

When it wasn't kite-flying weather, or the sea was too cold or rough, my hope was to be asked to join a tennis game on the grass at the Meadow Club, founded in 1887, which, with the Maidstone Club, its counterpart in East Hampton, is certainly the toniest facility on the South Fork. The members at both clubs are required to wear white. Andre Agassi, noted for his flamboyant tennis outfits, would have trouble setting foot on their courts. Some of the courts at the Meadow Club are better than others. Ridges build up on the base-lines, especially on the outer courts, which is of particular advantage to the powerful servers, one of whom told me it was like being up on a pitcher's mound. It was almost impossible to break serve. The worst courts are referred to as the "Cow Pasture." For many years, the Southampton Invitational was held at the Meadow Club, attracting almost all the top players, and they would moo loudly if required to play out there. I mentioned this in an article for *Sports Illustrated* and got in trouble with the club hierarchy. The score of one of the sets I watched (this before the advent of tie-breakers) was 31–29!

Sometimes I went to play golf at the National Golf Links of Southampton, one of the two great courses of the area. The other is the Shinnecock Golf Course, one of the oldest in the United States, built in 1891, and on which the U. S. Open was played in 1896 and 1986. A boom-period tycoon, Charles B. MacDonald, was the founder of the

National. Some of the holes on the course are patterned after those he had played abroad and admired—the Redon from North Berwick, the famous Road Hole of St. Andrews, with the deep potholes. Along the right fairway at the National a line of trees stands in for the railroad tracks of the Road Hole. MacDonald ran his club with an iron hand. A member would say, "Lord, there ought to be a place in the clubhouse where a fellow could play a spot of bridge," and if MacDonald happened to be within earshot, soon enough a room would be attached to the clubhouse and the bill for the construction sent to the bridge enthusiast.

The next year, we moved away from the tennis and the golf, back closer to the sea, even farther east in Southampton, to a beach house off Fowler Lane. We shared it that summer with another couple; the husband was a splendid outdoor cook, and I remember the sweet smell of the fire drifting up from the beach, and how later, swimming far out in the black sea, under a moonless sky, it was the fire, its sparks like fireflies, that guided us shoreward. It may have been the summer of *Jaws*, I've forgotten, but we stayed out in the water only long enough for our imaginations to take over and hasten us back through the surf-line until we reached down and felt the soft sand underfoot.

We kept moving eastward over the summers— the next time a big jump to Amagansett, the township just beyond East Hampton on the way to Montauk. For a number of years we lived on the curve of Gardiner's Bay in what everyone called the "domed house," for its roof, which looked like the observatory of a large astronomical telescope but was, in fact, the top of a silo trucked in from farm country and set atop the living-room section of the house. From the porch we looked out over the bay, across Cartright Shoals to Gardiner's Island, a mile or so away, its windmill clearly visible. The legend was that in the old days when the windmill sails were turned to make a cross, it meant that pirates were at hand and it was best to stay clear.

Gardiner's Island is one of the great sights in the Hamptons. Six miles long and three miles wide, it is, however, private property, and can't be visited unless permission is given, which is rare. Thus the island has remained very much the same over the centuries—a large stand of old-growth white oak known as Bostwick Wood, ponds, salt marshes, meadows like Scottish moors. It has a considerable wildlife population—wild turkeys, pheasant, deer. In past years it has been stocked with additional game and on occasion rented out for shooting parties allowed to blast away at just about anything from dawn to dusk. Ernest Hemingway told me years ago that he had been on one of these shoots with Winston Guest and that the first shot of the day was at the twin glare of a deer's eyes, which, unwavering as the rifle shot echoed across the meadows, turned out to be the headlights of a car across the Sound on the Connecticut shore.

The island has been in the Gardiner family's hands since 1639, when it was bought by Lion Gardiner from the Montauk Indians—by one account for a coat and a dog. By a royal grant bestowed by Charles I, the family was given the right to possess it forever. The present owner, Robert ("Bobby") David Lion Gardiner, is fond of pointing out that it is the oldest continuous royal grant in the New World and that it gives him the right to try a man on the island and hang him without interference from, say, the Suffolk County Police Department. He says things like, "The Gardiners were rich a hundred and fifty years before the United States existed."

We kept a creaky Boston-whaler-like boat at the Devon Yacht Club, in which we could on occasion cross the bay and venture illegally and nervously onto the island to relish its quiet woods, keeping an eye out not only for the caretaker, by all accounts a rough customer, but also, when we came out onto the headlands, for Bobby Gardiner himself. He often patrols the waters around the island in a sleek craft that carries a small pirate flag snapping from a stay.

It was best to persuade Bobby to give us a legal tour of the island, which he sometimes did, driving us around in whirlwind fashion in a battle-scarred Jeep. As we rattled along, plunging through bushes, overhead branches slapping against the windshield, he would keep up a steady commentary on the history of the island and his forebears. I remember him telling us about Julia Gardiner, a beauty known as the "Rose of Long Island" who married President John Tyler, a wid-

ower thirty years her senior. She was the one who introduced dancing to the White House and initiated the custom of playing "Hail to the Chief" whenever her husband appeared.

Bobby once took us to the site of Captain Kidd's treasure, supposedly buried by the pirate in 1699. He pointed offshore to where Sir Thomas "Kiss Me" Hardy had anchored his fleet during the War of 1812. I wanted to say that a crusty English naval historian had complained to me that it was absurd to think that Admiral Nelson, however badly he felt, would ask a flag officer to *kiss* him. Nonsense! What, mortally wounded, he had undoubtedly said at the Battle of Trafalgar was "Kismet, Hardy!" Fate, Hardy!

It was impossible to suggest this to our host since he was never one to be interrupted. We tore around the island. He was charmingly possessive about his property. If pheasants flew up, he'd invariably cry, "There go my pheasants!" A deer startled by our helter-skelter rush through Bostwick Wood would be claimed: "There goes my deer!" It was the same with everything: my osprey, my wild turkeys, my white oaks, on and on. One evening, at the cocktail hour at home, looking across the bay, smooth as glass, I fancied importing a rhinoceros, unloading it at night from a barge onto Gardiner's Island, and imagining it crashing through the bushes at the approach of Bobby's Jeep and what he would say as it came into view. "Here comes my . . . !"

Down the curve of the bay from where we lived and in violent contrast to the natural wonder of Gardiner's Island was the deserted Smith Meal Company factory, a gigantic relic of the days when Gardiner's Bay was the center of the menhaden industry. In 1898 over two hundred sailing boats and two dozen steam vessels set the seines for menhaden and brought them to Smith Meal and the smaller nearby factories known as "pot works." The produce was processed into glue and fertilizer. It was a lucrative business—the area was known as Promised Land. Then the huge menhaden schools were over-fished. The factories closed down.

Eventually, we moved from Amagansett back west again—to Wainscott. We lived at the end of Town Line Road, which is the dividing line between East Hampton and Southampton. There's not much to the village—a one-room school-house, a white-painted community house, and old homesteads here and there on the potato-field landscape, each protected by a grove of oak trees. Our house was just back from the sea. We started the big fireworks shows one summer in that house. My friends the Gruccis (the "First Family of Fireworks") came up from Bellport with an assort-ment of professional fireworks in mid-July. We set the mortars in the dunes. Sometimes we let the guests do the firing; they would crouch as if feed-ing a leopard to touch off the fuse with a flare. Once, I remember, the first shell of the evening opened high up—white magnesium—and it illu-minated just for an instant an owl, tossed briefly by the concussion before we watched it flap off into the darkness. Finally the fireworks shows became too popular—hundreds coming across the potato fields to watch—and the venue was shifted to Three Mile Harbor and the fireworks shot off barges. The show is now held annually to benefit Anthony Biddle Duke's remarkable institution for city kids—Boys and Girls Harbor.

In 1985, about a mile west of Town Line Road, we finally bought a home—a large farmhouse in Sagaponack on Sagg Main Street with a barn, a stand of bamboo, and potato fields out back. Most of the houses along Sagg Main were built in the nineteenth century with porches out front so the owners could sit in their rocking chairs and watch who was passing by. The houses are quite close together—a throwback to the times when it was important to yell to your neighbor that a wolf had been spotted. Next door, our neighbors were the novelist, Kurt Vonnegut, and his wife, Jill Krementz. The stretch of Sagg Main to the sea, only a couple of miles, has had an astonishing number of writers and artists living along its length—besides the Vonneguts, Peter Matthiessen, John Irving, James Jones, Kaylie Jones, Linda Francke, Peter Tompkins, Truman Capote, Jack Dunphy, Caroline Kennedy Schlossberg, Alfred Wright, Fred Seidel, and James Salter are the ones who come to mind, as well as Bob Dash, the painter, and Charles Addams, *The New Yorker* cartoonist.

The rialto for this crowd is the pint-sized Sagg General Store, which also serves as a post office. I often run into Kurt Vonnegut on his way to get his morning paper. We stop and chat about the model airplanes with their whiny gnat-buzz engines that fly over our houses on weekends. The model air-plane club meets at the Potter Farm and its grass airstrip. We plot our various strategies to knock their planes out of the sky. Kurt's is that he will arrange for a miniature submarine to be settled into his swimming pool so that it can rise up from the depths, fire off its heat-seeking missiles, and then submerge from sight. My fancy is this: I have an English friend who trains falcons; my notion is to get him to bring his birds to Sagaponack, hide them in the hedgerows, and then send them aloft to duel with the model airplanes that the subma-rine's heat-seeking missiles have missed and spin them out of the sky. Kurt and I whisper on Sagg Main like the conspirators we are.

If the writers of the Hamptons have dispropor-tionately deposited themselves along Sagg Main, the same can be said of the artists and the village of Springs near the Accabonac marshes. I hadn't realized until recently when I read Jason Epstein and Elizabeth Barlow's *East Hampton: A History and Guide* that the artists came to the Hamptons in two waves, the first in the 1870s, when a large number appeared as part of a project initiated by *Scribner's* magazine to have representations done of every township in Long Island. The painters commis-sioned to do this were all members of the Tile Club, so called because its members were asked to decorate a tile at their weekly meetings. They included Winslow Homer, Childe Hassam, and Thomas Moran. Moran, who was a protégé of John Ruskin, painted the enormous canvases of Yosemite and Yellowstone that were rolled out on the floors of Congress, influencing the legislatures to estab-lish the National Parks system. In East Hampton, Moran kept a gondola (supposedly it once belonged to Robert Browning) on Hook Pond with a Montauk Indian employed as a gondolier. At the time of the *Scribner's* magazine commission, many of the artists stayed in a boarding house called Rowdy Hall, from where, after a night of revelry, they would fan out into the fields with their easels and umbrellas. These worthies had a lot to do with spreading the word, vocally and through their work, about the scenic pleasures of the area.

The second wave of artists came in the late 1940s, the first of them Jackson Pollock and Robert Motherwell, followed by Willem de Kooning, Ibram Lassaw, Norman Bluhm, Franz Kline, John Brooks, Larry Rivers, Alfonso Ossorio, and Wilfred Zogbaum. Practitioners of the Abstract Expressionist school, they moved into early farmhouses, carpetless and airy. I always heard it was the "magical" light that hung over the potato fields that drew painters there, but it is hard to see its influence in their work. Jackson Pollock was the greatest of them. He died along with a young woman friend when he lost control of his car at night on the Fireplace–Springs Road near Three Mile Harbor. The car horn, stuck in the force of the crash, was still sounding when they were found. He is buried in the Green River Cemetery in Springs, his grave marked by an enormous boulder appropriately enough referred to by geologists as an "erratic"—the name given mammoth rocks pushed down from the northeast by glaciers and found as an occasional outcrop on the flat farmlands. Many fellow artists have bought plots in that same cemetery—so many that someone once quipped, "Everyone's dying to get into Green River Cemetery."

Everybody has a preference. Sometimes I wish we had continued renting so that we could have savored other areas of the Hamptons—Sag Harbor, Montauk, Water Mill. I'm not sure, though, that I would like to have been around in the earliest days of the Hamptons. At the time of the Revolution it must have been one of the sleepiest corners of the new Republic: matters brought up at town meetings in East Hampton were of such moment as what color to paint the meeting house, or whether to put up guideposts to Sag Harbor. In 1810 (and one likes to think after considerable soul-searching), it was decided "to get a box made in the gallery with a hole in it for Mr. Dimon to put his Psalm book and pitch pipe in."

About the only excitement of those times—short of the Sunday sermon (Lyman Beecher, the father of Harriet Beecher Stowe, was East Hampton's spirited preacher) was the whaling activity. Whales were so plentiful that they floated ashore like driftwood. In fact, they were called as such: drift whales. In 1702 a young woman riding her horse on the beach between East Hampton and East Mecox counted thirteen whales that had drifted ashore. The last whale was taken in the Atlantic off Amagansett on February 22, 1907. Its skeleton is the one that hangs from the roof of the Oceanic Hall of Fishes in New York City's American Museum of Natural History.

If the fishing has changed over the years, so has the topography of the land. In a sense it is ironic that old-timers decry the steady disappearance of the potato fields to development. At the turn of the century the land was given over to diversified farming; the boundaries that marked off a farmer's property were made of privet hedges. Then shortly after World War I, a number of Polish farmers settled in the Hamptons and in the rich (so-called Bridgehampton loam) soil commenced the kind of farming they had practiced in their homeland. The privet hedges were torn down (much to the dismay of both conservationists and hunters who thought the bird populations would be affected), and the subsistence farming gave way to the vast, unbroken acreage of potato fields. Now the potato fields are being overrun by examples of modern architecture at its most imaginative—hard-edged abstract sculptures, which Paul Goldberger of *The New York Times* describes as "architecture of shrill egotism—whose arrogance says as much about its owners' aesthetic tastes as about the extent of their responsibilities to the land on which they have settled."

However much the landscape is given over to change, each of the communities' many constituents—Bonakers (the term for the baymen who make their living from the fish and shellfish), farmers, the well-to-do, the arrivistes, the artists—each has kept a strong sense of identity. The haute monde of Southampton and East Hampton, a few miles apart, pride themselves on the differences between the two communities, though in fact its members come from exactly the same sources in New York City—from its banks, its financial markets, its benefit galas, its fancier restaurants, its clubs. The East Hampton contingent thinks of itself as being conservative in manner and dress, shy of the public gaze, scornful of ostentation, and quite snooty about the rather more worldly behavior of their bloodlines down the road in Southampton.

Until quite recently, a professional photographer stood outside the entrance of the posh Southampton Bathing Corporation (known locally as the Beach Club) to catch the arrival of members for immortalization in the society pages of *Town and Country, Harper's Bazaar,* and *Vogue.* Aware of this, the majority of the members dressed hardly for the ocean but made their entrances preened in blazers and summer dresses for veranda lunches.

The artistic community didn't care a jot about this sort of thing, with the possible exception of Truman Capote. He could not resist a dig or two at the Southampton social scene, especially when fortified with drink. On one occasion for a black–tie Southampton dinner, he arrived wearing a pith helmet, which he wore through the evening. A lot of burglaries were being committed in the community at the time. Capote's reasoning was that a burglar peering through a window and casing the place might be scared off because it was apparent a policeman had been invited to dinner and might well be staying on as an overnight guest. He did not seem at all deterred by the fact that his diminutive form, topped by the pith helmet, did not give the slightest impression of a law–enforcement official. At one point during the dinner, he stood up in his chair to toast the hostess, whom he admired. He said something to the effect: "Well, here's to all you superficial jerks who don't appreciate the only non–superficial person in the place." I sometimes saw Capote at the Sagaponack General Store. Often he drove up in a convertible with the top down, his bulldog sitting next to him in the front seat. Their heads just barely showed above the dashboard. Seen from head–on, it was hard to tell which one was driving.

One of the pleasures of Sagaponack was to drive or bicycle to the tennis courts in the Georgica Association, a private enclave of houses set in the thick woods around Georgica Pond. At the western end of the courts is the Wainscott windmill. Like many other windmills in the Hamptons it has had a surprisingly peripatetic existence. Originally built in Southampton in 1813, it was moved to Wainscott in 1852. Then, purchased by a Montauk resident, it was attached to a house there and used as a sitting room. When the Montauk area was appropriated by the U. S. military during World War II, the Georgica Association acquired it and set it back in the same vicinity from where it had left about a hundred years before. I never could play in its shadow without thinking of my own peripatetic movements through the Hamptons.

This has been a personalized sketch of the Hampton communities. There is not enough about Westhampton, which I have visited on occasion but do not know well. I associate Westhampton with Budd Schulberg, who wrote *Waterfront* and *What Makes Sammy Run?*, among other fine novels. He keeps swans in the canal off his property. They come hissing out of the water onto the lawn bent on mischief when I drop in to say hello. I have taken refuge in his studio with its great boxing posters which I look at carefully, keeping a wary eye on the door—not the best vantage point from which to assess a community!

There are other omissions. There is not enough about the Walking Dunes of Napeague, so called because their nearly accreted sands make them shift and move, even burying trees in their slow passage, or the Montauk Lighthouse and the creeping erosion that will topple it into the sea one day, making true George Washington's prophecy when it was built that it would last two hundred years. Nor is there anything about the long V–shaped flights of Canada geese, or the time the golden plovers on their way to Patagonia from the Arctic took over a potato field in Sagaponack for a few days, or the great storms that come in the fall and carve away the beaches so that in Westhampton the stilt houses, fragile and doomed, stand away from the beaches in the sea like miniature oil rigs. There should have been mention of the bluefish runs in August in Gardiner's Bay, the terns fluttering about the water that churns from the feeding fish below; or standing waist–deep and with the long casting rods flinging the plugs beyond the surf–line for striped bass. There could have been more about the architecture—the many–gabled stately home on Ox Pasture Road in Southampton, where the Duchess of Marlborough lived her summers, or the Gothic castle that Barry Trupin, the real–estate syndicator, tried to build where the old DuPont place had stood on Dune Road, before he was shut down by Southampton

because its turrets thrust higher than the town ordinances allowed. And what about the American Hotel in Sag Harbor, the Parrish Art Museum in Southampton, the Marine Museum in Amagansett with its ingenious device for skinning eels, Guild Hall, with its summer stock productions, the Candy Kitchen in Bridgehampton which has been serving its ice cream concoctions for sixty years. There could have been a lament about the hours car-bound on the Long Island Expressway, sometimes as many as four or five on a Friday, before one crept across the Shinnecock Canal, and how on weekends they say it's wise to pack a lunch if one plans to cross the Montauk Highway at noon. There could have been notice of the Hampton Horse show, the Fourth of July parades. There is nothing about the annual Writers and Artists softball game in East Hampton and the time Paul Simon, batting left-handed, knocked in Christopher Reeves, sliding bare-chested across the plate from second base with the winning run; or how Mort Zuckerman, the pitcher, cut off the throw coming in from the outfield that might have caught Reeves, so that for a while we referred to him as "Cut-Off" Mort until the anguish of the loss dissipated. There is not enough space to describe fully other notable sporting events, two of them, in particular, that Dan Rattiner of *Dan's Papers*, a popular tract distributed free through the Hamptons, holds every year. One of them is a kite-flying competition on Peter's Pond Beach where twenty-four prizes are awarded by four judges, all of whom traditionally have the same first name; one year a winner flew a six-foot-long hypodermic needle that darted maniacally above the beach. The other event is *Dan's Papers'* "Flight to Portugal," which takes place off the Montauk cliffs—launching a glider or rubber-band-powered model aircraft (the minimum length is three feet) far enough out over the Atlantic to beat the competition; the judges this time are Grumman Aerospace officials, undoubtedly with different first names, as well as the Coast Guard, which is also charged with recovering contraptions landing out beyond the breakers. Why not more about the record-holder for distance, a homemade model with propellers fore and aft powered by rubber bands, and when the front one quit, the back one kicked in and between them they took the plane out about a half mile; and how beforehand the contestants sit cross-legged at the cliff edge and offer up Buddhist chants (*oooom!*) to imbue their machines with the Way.

A prayer seems an appropriate place to conclude. It should only be added that one of the benefits of photography, especially in professional hands, is that it elicits an emotional response without the clumsy apparatus of words. So to paraphrase John Wesley's, "though I am always in haste, I am never in a hurry," let us hasten to dally in a perusal of the visual.

—*George Plimpton*
Sagaponock, Long Island

THE HAMPTONS

Above: Town Marine Museum, Amagansett.

Opposite: Residence (former home of "beer baron" John L. Nostrand),
built circa 1880, Shelter Island.

Page 25: Oceanfront patio, East Hampton.

Above and opposite: Clubhouse, Shinnecock Hills Golf Club.

Pages 30–31: Guesthouse, built circa 1910, Southampton.

Above: An artist's garden, Sagaponack.

Opposite: Shingle-style cottage, East Hampton.

Above: Old Schoolhouse Museum, built circa 1822, Quogue.

Opposite: Roman Caesars, The Parrish Art Museum,
opened 1898, Southampton.

Opposite: Hedge–lined private drive, East Hampton.

Page 38, top: Meadow, Amagansett; bottom: Fields of gold, East Hampton.

Page 39, top: Potato field and barn, Bridgehampton; bottom: Robert Appleton House, built 1918, East Hampton.

Above: Silos, Sagaponack.

Opposite: Old Whalers Church, built circa 1843–1844, Sag Harbor. The 165–foot steeple of this Egyptian revival–style church was toppled during the 1938 hurricane.

Pages 40–41: Dune Walk, Southampton.

Gazebo, Southampton.

View of Peconic Bay, Shelter Island.

Opposite: Residence, Southampton.

Page 48: Residence, East Hampton.

Page 49: Saint Andrew's Dune Church,
built circa 1851, Southampton.

Above: Pickets and privets, East Hampton.

Opposite: Garden, Georgica.

Pages 52–53: Residence, designed by Gwathmey Siegel & Associates, 1983, Amagansett.

Above: Residence, designed by Nagel and Lesser, 1988, East Hampton.

Opposite: Residence, designed by Charles Gwathmey, 1967, Amagansett.

Pages 56–57: Lap pool, designed by Aqua–Qual, Bridgehampton.

Entrance, Villa Maria Convent, Water Mill.

Gates and fences. Clockwise from top left: Amagansett,
Sag Harbor, Southampton, Sag Harbor.

Tall ship, Gardiners Bay.

Beach erosion, Westhampton Beach.

Culver's Bathing Pavilion, built circa 1900–1901,
Main Beach, East Hampton.

Above: Fishing-boat dock, Montauk Harbor.

Opposite: Lawn sculpture, Shelter Island.

Pages 64–65: Residence, Montauk.

Pages 68–69: Annual Blessing of the Fleet celebration, Montauk.

Above: Lazy Point, Napeague.

Opposite: Georgica Beach, East Hampton.

Pages 70–71: Georgica Beach jetty, East Hampton.

Water Mill Museum, built circa 1644–1645.

Residence, East Quogue.

Above: Teepee, Shinnecock reservation, Southampton.

Pages 78–79: South End Cemetery, the oldest cemetery in East
Hampton, with grave markers dating from the seventeenth century.

Above: Croquet court, Southampton.

Opposite: Annual Hampton Classic horse show, Bridgehampton.

Above and opposite: Hampton Classic horse show, Bridgehampton.

Top left: Tractor, Southampton; top right: The musketeers at Casa Basso restaurant, Westhampton; bottom left: "Manny Quinn" traffic–violation deterrent, East Hampton; bottom right: Duck farm landmark, Hampton Bays.

Annual Native–American powwow,
Shinnecock reservation, Southampton.

Opposite: View from residence, Montauk.

Page 88: Montauk Harbor.

Page 89: Fishing buoys, East Hampton.

Above: Rooftops, Free Library, East Hampton.

Opposite: Windmill, built circa 1712–1714, Southampton College.

Above: Entrance gate, Water Mill.

Opposite: Residence, East Hampton.

Pages 94–95: Beach house and walk, Amagansett.

Opposite: Residence, East Hampton.

Page 96: Sagaponack Schoolhouse,
built 1885, Sagaponack.

Page 97: Farm, Water Mill.

Pages 100–101: Farmland and residence, Water Mill.

Amagansett Market.

Top left: Amagansett Market.
Top right: Roadside vegetable stand, Bridgehampton.
Bottom left: Fall harvest, Bridgehampton.
Bottom right: Summer harvest, Bridgehampton.

Opposite: Clinton Academy, the first accredited high school in New York State, built circa 1784–1785, East Hampton.

Pages 104–105: Field, Wainscott.

Page 106: Town pond, Main Street, East Hampton.

Page 107: Bird sanctuary, East Hampton.

Above: Sunstone, residence, East Quogue.

Opposite: Quogue Library, built 1897.

Pages 112–113: Hook Mill, built circa 1806, East Hampton.

Above: Halsey House, the oldest house in Southampton and the oldest English saltbox–style house in New York State, built circa 1648.

Opposite: Blacksmith, apothecary, and cobbler replica shops, Southampton Historical Society complex.

Above: Window flower box, Quogue.

Opposite: Second House Museum, the oldest
house in Montauk, built circa 1746.

Opposite: Meadow, Montauk Highway, East Hampton.

Pages 120–121: Annual Bastille Day celebration,
Three Mile Harbor, East Hampton.

Above: Garden gates, Bridgehampton.

Opposite: The Inn at Quogue.

Pages 124–125: Sunrise, Wainscott.

Above: Amagansett Market.

Opposite: I Santi restaurant, Water Mill.

Page 126: Lobster Roll restaurant, Napeague.

Page 127: Movie theater, Westhampton.

Guild Hall, museum and theater complex,
built 1930, East Hampton.

Top left: Quogue Street Foods, Quogue.
Top right: Urban Archaeology, Bridgehampton.
Bottom left: The Springs General Store, East Hampton Springs.

Bottom right: Sagaponack General Store, built circa 1885, Sagaponack.

The American Hotel, built circa 1846, Sag Harbor.

Above: Village shops, Main Street, Sag Harbor.

Opposite: Saks Fifth Avenue, Southampton.

Pages 136–137: Victorian houses, Shelter Island.

Pages 138–139: Residence, designed by Gwathmey
Siegel & Associates, 1986, East Hampton.

Above: Rose garden, Southampton.

Opposite: Ocean estate, Southampton.

Pages 142–143: Sunstone, residence, East Quogue.

Opposite: Specimen garden, East Hampton.

Pages 146–147: By the Way, residence, Southampton.

Gray Gardens, spring (above) and summer (opposite), East Hampton.

150

Above: Sheltered garden, Bridgehampton.

Opposite: Bridle path, Southampton.

Opposite: LongHouse, residence, East Hampton.

Pages 152–153: Cemetery, Bridgehampton.

Pages 154–155: Residence, designed by Richard Meier, 1969, East Hampton.

Top: LongHouse interior, East Hampton.

Bottom: Residence interior, Southampton.

Residence interior, Water Mill.

Residence, Southampton.

Residence, East Hampton.

Opposite: Residence, East Hampton.

Pages 162–163: Former Nostrand residence
and boathouse, Shelter Island.

Automobile auction, East Hampton.

Above: Along Montauk Highway.

Pages 168–169: Private garden, Bridgehampton.

Above: Greenhouse mums, Bridgehampton.

Opposite: Roadside stand, Bridgehampton.

Pages 172–173: Home Sweet Home farmhouse and gristmill, East Hampton.

Hither Lane, summer (above) and winter (opposite), East Hampton.

175

Above: The Hampton Jitney bus line.

Opposite: Horse farm, Southampton.

Most Holy Trinity Church (formerly Saint
Philomena), built circa 1894, East Hampton.

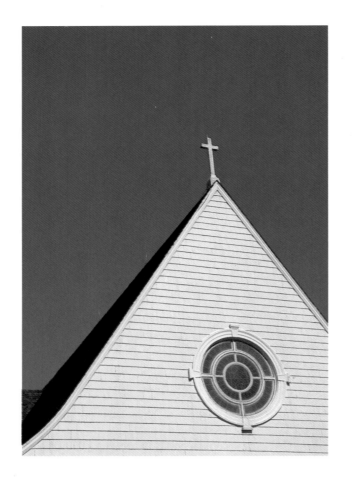

Top left: Queen of the Most Holy Rosary Church, built 1915, Bridgehampton; top right: Clubhouse, Shinnecock Hills Golf Club; bottom left: Bell tower, Quogue; bottom right: Weather vane, Amagansett.

Mill and barn, Shelter Island.

182

Residence, East Hampton.

Above: Ditch Plains, Montauk.

Opposite: Quogue Canal.

Pages 184–185: Residence, Shelter Island.

Page 186: Residence, Southampton.

Page 187: Residence, Southampton.

Dunes, Amagansett.

Above: Goldenrod, Wyandanch Beach, Southampton.

Opposite: Two Holes of Water, East Hampton.

Wildflowers, Montauk Highway, Bridgehampton.

Above: Snapdragons, Southampton.

Pages 196–197: Ditch Plains, Montauk.

Above: Residence, Wainscott Beach.

Opposite: Georgica Beach, East Hampton.

Above: Residence, Montauk.

Opposite: Boardwalk, Dune Road, Southampton.

Pages 202–203: Residence, East Hampton.

Above: Atlantic Beach, Amagansett.

Opposite: Lifeguard tower, Southampton.

Pages 206–207: Montauk Lighthouse, commissioned by President George Washington in 1795.

Page 208: Wainscott Beach.

204

ACKNOWLEDGMENTS

I wish to thank the following individuals and institutions who helped to bring this book to fruition: Millie Andrews and the Southampton Chamber of Commerce, Richard Auer, John Barham, Linda and Curt Bawden, Arthur Beckenstein, Sig Bergamin, Kerry Botz, Ben Bradlee and Sally Quinn, Tom Britt, Burton and Susan Brous, George Caldwell, George Castello, Richard Cirringione, Randy Correll, Joanne Creveling, Robert Dash, Cindy and Ray Eldridge, Norman and Susan Ember, Tom Fallon, Robert Fallon, Mrs. Eugene Fudderman, Paul Goertz, Karen Gomes and Italian *Vogue*, Gordon Campbell Gray, Bernard Green, Janusz Grzeczny, Charles Gwathmey, John Huszar, Anthony Ingrao, Norman Jaffe, William Jones, Ed, Bob, and Bill Kaminski of Aqua-Qual Swimming Pools of Farmingdale, Carolyn Kelly, Dorothy King and the East Hampton Free Library, Calvin and Kelly Klein, Diane Koster, Richard Kozusko, Jack Larsen and The LongHouse Foundation, Armand LeGardeur, Susan Magrino, Karen and Gary Mark, Richard Meier, Lee Mindel and Shelton, Mindel, and Associates, Architects, Tom Neely and the Hampton Jitney, Susan Peters, John Picucci, Mary Pogacich, Terry Rogers, Joe Roman, Patricia Ross, Mr. and Mrs. Renny Saltzman, Mr. and Mrs. Virgil Sherrill, Robert A. M. Stern, Martha Stewart, Sandy and Dick Tarlow, William Timm, and Massimo and Lella Vignelli.

A special thanks to John Brancati, Jennifer Condon, Robert Janjigian, Charles Miers, and Elizabeth White, at Rizzoli, and to Gilda Hannah, who designed this book.

Finally, thanks to Ken Roberts Detelich for his continual support.